GREASY LUCK

UNDER SAIL

A Yankee whaling barque of the fifties

GREASY LUCK

A WHALING SKETCH BOOK
by
GORDON GRANT

DOVER PUBLICATIONS, INC.
MINEOLA, NEW YORK

Bibliographical Note

This Dover edition, first published in 2004, is an unabridged republication of the work first published by William Farquhar Payson, New York, in 1932. We have slightly reduced the size of this edition and have removed the tinted background of the plates.

Library of Congress Cataloging-in-Publication Data

Grant, Gordon, 1875–1962.
  Greasy luck : a whaling sketchbook / Gordon Grant.
    p. cm.
  Originally published: New York : William Farquhar Payson, 1932.
  ISBN 0-486-43741-8 (pbk.)
    1. Grant, Gordon, 1875–1962. 2. Whaling in art. I. Title.

NC139.G68A4 2004
741'.092—dc22

2004049367

Manufactured in the United States of America
Dover Publications, Inc., 31 East 2nd Street, Mineola, N.Y. 11501

TO

MY WIFE

a lover of ships

The author gratefully acknowledges his debt to
FRANK WOOD and WILLIAM H. TRIPP of the
Whaling Museum of New Bedford, for their
splendid cooperation—and to CLIFFORD
W. ASHLEY and his most admirable
book *"The Yankee Whaler"*

FOREWORD

Turning the pages of Gordon Grant's pictured story of whaling, it suddenly struck me that the task of writing an introduction had certain unusual features. Acting as a liaison officer between Captain Ahab of the whaling ship *Pequod* and the sheltered generation of 1932, it is necessary to bear in mind that most members of this generation are unaware that whaling is still an industry. They imagine it as part of the closed book of New England maritime history. They regard it romantically, and the ancient masthead shout, "Thar she blows!" is familiar to the ladies and gentlemen who patronize the fast Atlantic ferries. Whaling, in short, has become an antique interest, and visitors to New Bedford may study the whole business in the collection of the Old Dartmouth Historical Society.

The difference between this adventurous and romantic calling and the modern whaleship is precisely the difference between pig-sticking as practised by army officers in India and the stock-yards of Chicago and Argentina. Making all allowance for the New Englander's passion for gain, there had to be some sporting instinct to send men out on "lays" instead of wages, and to make them follow, year after year, so dangerous a trade. It was only when another sporting chance came along, the chance of the golden west, of striking further and further beyond the ranges, that the New Englanders abandoned the whaling to foreigners. The interest our antiquarians have in whaling is therefore a sound one. It was a manifestation of the pioneer mentality; and when that mentality was directed into other channels, whaling lost prestige and became as prosaic as cod-fishing in modern times.

It might be mentioned here that the two instincts of civilized man—to make a sport of his necessities, and then by quantity production in factories to divorce all sport from his necessities—have been spectacularly illustrated in the evolution of whaling from a sport for heroes into a humdrum manifestation of big business. Efficiency has never been so swiftly or so deplorably justified. At one end of the scale we have Captain Ahab devoting all his life to the pursuit of a mythological cetacean, the White Whale. At the other, in 1932, we have British and Scandinavian whaling factories, twin screw, oil-burning vessels of 14,000 tons, capable of pursuing whales of all species in high speed motor whaleboats fitted with guns and bombs, with air pumps which inflate the dead whale so that it will float until needed. These ships have a specially designed stern slipway, up which the entire carcase of a 100 ton whale can be hauled from the water to the blubber deck. When the blubber has been removed the carcase is sawn by machinery into sections and lowered to the meat deck. Nothing of the animal is wasted. A packing factory on board cans and packs the products ready for discharging at a convenient port into freight steamers. Fuel-oil and water, which is distilled on board, supplies a whole fleet of auxiliary whaling vessels.

Here we behold the modern commercial and mechanical genius at its peak. It is so efficient that unless some legislative action is taken, whales will become extinct. In two years these vessels have obtained more oil and have killed more whales than the old American whalers took from the sea in half a century.

It is true, as a recent author contends, that whaling is not properly described as fishing. The whale is an animal, and his pursuit is a form of hunting. In Gordon Grant's drawings the whole art and craft of catching whales is most lucidly and dramatically set forth. It is sport because the hunters risked their lives when the harpoon left the boatsteerer's hands to plunge into the whale's carcase. They were in the most dire peril of a "stove" or a "chawed" boat until the animal's terrific struggles were ended by the thrust of a lance through his vitals. In modern whaling the operatives are in no more danger than the person who slits the jugular veins of the hogs suspended by their hind legs on a moving chain in a Chicago abattoir. I doubt exceedingly whether these modern whalers will ever have any songs or traditions. All too soon they will, as I understand it, have no more whales. They will have become history themselves without ever having become known to the public. If by chance the captain of the *Vikingen,* of the Viking Whaling Company, Limited, of London, ever meets Moby Dick, he will order full speed ahead on his 4300 horsepower and overhaul the White Whale in a few hours. A few days later he will be in sealed cans.

Ships, and especially sailing craft, are the unhappy victims of artists who know more about pretty pictures than ships. They take quite felonious liberties with the craft and the men they depict. In "Greasy Luck" however, you will find the most austere fidelity to the truth combined with what to me is a most satisfying vivacity of presentation. I commend to your notice the lowered whaleboat on page 59 as an example of what I mean. Such a boat was an instrument to which men entrusted their lives and fortunes. It was the product of deep thought and shrewd designing for a century. It was, as one writer says, "sharp and clean-cut as a dolphin" with "a duck-like capacity to top the oncoming waves, so that it will dryly ride where ordinary boats would fill. . . . Here we have a boat that two men may lift, and which will make ten miles an hour in dead chase by the oars alone." Such a craft has a beauty of its own, not to be found in pleasure craft. The same boat is shown at a dramatic moment of "A Nantucket Sleigh Ride" on page 75.

It appears to me that Mr. Grant has made a definitive and conclusive contribution to Whaliana. If the whales go the way of the buffalo of North America, we shall depend on this book for a lively conception of the ancient sport. Ships and wild animals, it has been remarked, have a hard and tragic ending. This book will preserve for posterity the spiritual as well as the material glories of the whaler's life.

William McFee

LIST OF PLATES

Under Sail		*Frontispiece*
Fitting Out		*Facing Page* 2
Hoisting Topsails		4
Choosing Boats' Crews		6
A Harangue from the Captain		8
Getting in the Mainsail		10
Stowing the Outer Jib		12
A Typical Bow		14
A Typical Stern		16
The Deck		18
The Whaleboat		20
A Boat on the Cranes		22
Spare Boats		24
Harpoons		26
The Wheel		28
The Foc's'le		30
The Windlass		32
The Galley		34
Types		36
The Blacksmith		38
The Cooper		40
Grinding Spades		42
Coiling Line Tubs		44
Ten Dollars Reward		46
Grub		48
Fresh Fish for the Cook to Spoil		50
Whales		52
Whales		54
The Masthead		56
Lowering		58
A Race Under Sail		60

Waifing . . . . *Facing Page* 62

"Going On" 64

"Give it to him!" 66

Sounding 68

A Breach 70

A "Chawed" Boat 72

"A Nantucket Sleigh Ride" 74

Lancing 76

Towing to the Ship 78

Cutting-in Diagram 80

Removing the Lower Jaw 82

The Junk 84

Cutting In 86

The Blanket Piece Coming Aboard 88

Lowering into the Hold 90

Mincing 92

Trying Out 94

Bailing the Case 96

Cleaning Ship 98

Main Hatch Surgery 100

Boat Surgery 102

Ashore for Water 104

Having it Out 106

Recruiting on the Beach 108

A "Gam" 110

Song and Dance 112

Bumboats 114

Arctic Whaling 116

Whalebone 118

Cleaning Whalebone 120

Dead Man's Chest 122

Homeward Bound 124

"Scrimshaw" 126

SKETCHES

FITTING OUT

THE last few days prior to a ship's departure on a whaling voyage witnessed great activity along the wharves of all whaling ports: New Bedford, Fairhaven, Nantucket, Sag Harbor, Salem, and New London, to note but a few in New England; in Dundee, Scotland, and Bergen in Norway.

With the prospect of a voyage lasting perhaps three years, no item of gear for the ship or provision for the crew was overlooked.

On sailing day, with everything checked off and stowed below, the crew came aboard, the owners, their wives, and the townspeople crowded the wharf to cheer them on their way and wish them "Greasy Luck."

HOISTING TOPSAILS

THE work of the merchant ship sailor had but one object; to take the ship by the shortest route from port to port. The whaleman, on the other hand, in addition to his seamanship, was expert in the highly technical work of killing whales.

While the whaling skippers lacked the smartness of the clipper captains they were able, keen, and resourceful in emergencies that the merchant ship masters seldom, if ever, were called upon to face.

CHOOSING BOATS' CREWS

Soon after the ship was on her course the crew was mustered and divided into two watches—starboard and larboard—(the word "port" was not used in whaleships). This done, the boats' crews were chosen, consisting of an officer, harpooneer, and four men. The mates in turn took their pick of the men for their respective boats, subjected their choice to questions regarding former ships and experience, and an inspection of hands, feet, and muscular development—much like farmers at a cattle show.

The harpooneers were called "boatsteerers," which, to the landsman, is somewhat misleading.

The mate steered the boat until the harpooneer struck the whale. They thereupon changed places and the latter became "boatsteerer."

The boatsteerers ranked next to the officers,—were quartered aft, and had a separate mess.

A HARANGUE FROM THE CAPTAIN

THE watches and boats' crews chosen, the captain called for attention and delivered himself of a speech. The gist of his message did not vary much from that of all other whaling skippers and his delivery was more or less colourful according to his ability as an orator.

Running his eye from man to man, so that none escaped the implied meaning behind the glance, he would voice his thoughts substantially as follows:—"This ship is a whaler and we're out to kill whales. I tell you that now in case you might think you're aboard a yacht and came along for a picnic. I'm captain and these are my officers, and when an order is given I want to see some jumping. I don't want any loafers or grumblers. Loafers and grumblers only make trouble for themselves, and if any of you want trouble I'll see that you damned well get it. You'll get good food and all you need—so I don't want to hear any growling about that. I won't have any fighting or swearing. The sooner you fill the ship the sooner you'll get home:—and remember; there's only one captain aboard here and that's me. If anyone wants to dispute that I'll damned soon show him. That'll do——"

GETTING IN THE MAINSAIL

To THE watch, bending over the yard with nought between them and oblivion but a slender foot rope, this was no easy task even in a moderate wind. In a gale, with wet or frozen sails, the stowing of this huge expanse of thrashing canvas can be better imagined than described.

STOWING THE OUTER JIB

Gordon Grant

A TYPICAL BOW

HERE we have the bows of the barque "California" of New Bedford, built in the early eighteen forties.

Square-rigged whaling craft varied in size from two hundred and fifty to four hundred tons, seldom exceeding the latter figure.

Many were painted "frigate fashion" with black ports along the side—a relic of the days when merchant ships used this device to deceive pirates into the belief that they were heavily armed.

The whaler had a beauty peculiarly her own. She was rather a tubby little thing, but with much grace notwithstanding. She was held in supreme contempt by the officers and crews of her contemporaneous big sisters the flash clippers, who referred to her as "spouter" and "butcher shop."

A TYPICAL STERN

UNLIKE merchant ships, whalers had to keep their forward deck clear so that all space could be devoted to the "cutting in" and "trying out" of blubber.

The forward deck-house, characteristic of cargo carriers, which contained the gallery and crew's quarters, was moved far aft—half to starboard—half to larboard—with a deck overhead from which the quarter-boats were lowered.

The stern shown is that of "Lagoda," a half size model of which has been installed in the Whaling Museum in New Bedford.

THE DECK

THIS diagram shows the deck arrangement of "Lagoda" of New Bedford and was characteristic of all square-rigged whalers.

A—B—C—D—E—Boats hanging on the davits. Many ships did not swing a boat in the position of "B."

In their order the boats were named as follows:—"Bow"—"Starboard Bow"—"Waist"—"Larboard"—"Starboard." The latter was known as the captain's boat, though in later years the captain did not leave the ship.

The first mate had the larboard boat—second mate the waist—third mate the bow.

The senior boatsteerer took the starboard bow boat unless the ship carried a fourth mate.

F— Spare boats on the skids—or boat bridge.

G—The main hatch.

H—The try works.

J— The steering wheel.—To left of the wheel, the companion stairs to captain's quarters.

K—The galley.

L— The "cutting-in" stage. At this point a section of the bulwarks was removed during cutting in.

M—The foc's'le hatch leading to crew's quarters below.

N—The windlass.

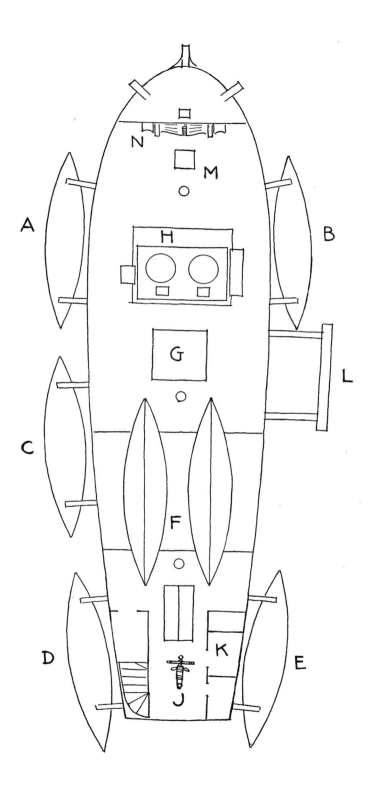

THE WHALEBOAT

BOATS varied from 28 to 30 feet in length, with a beam of 5½ to 6 feet.

A—Bow showing the "chocks," a channel in the stem through which the whale line ran. This was fitted with a bronze roller—or lined with sheet lead.

Through a hole across the chocks a slender spindle of wood was inserted—to be easily broken should necessity arise.

This "chock pin" kept the line from jumping out of its groove,—and was, moreover, when worn in the buttonhole ashore, the badge of the whaleman who had killed his whale.

B—Main line tub—containing 225 fathoms of whale line.

C—Reserve tub—holding from 75 to 125 fathoms.

D—Loggerhead—a heavy snubbing post around which the whale line ran from the tub and thence forward to the bow.

E—Mast step.

F—Padded notch in the edge of the forward box into which the harpooneer braced his thigh when darting his irons.

L—Centreboard.

Except when under sail the boat was propelled by five oars, and in order to balance the power from this unequal number, oars of different lengths were used.

G—Harpoon oar   16 feet long
H—Bow oar   17   "   "
I— Midship oar   18   "   "
J— Tub oar   17   "   "
K—After or stroke oar 16   "   "

Except when under sail the boat was steered by means of an oar over twenty feet long.

The complete equipment of a boat included paddles, harpoons, lances, spades, mast and sail, water and bread kegs, lantern, flares and waifs, and other small gear.

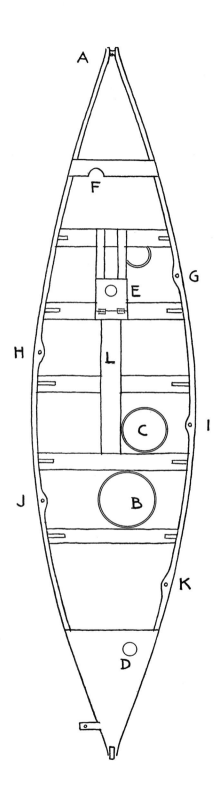

A BOAT ON THE CRANES

THE whaleboat was so lightly constructed that had it been allowed to hang by the hoisting tackle or "falls," there was danger of it "hogging" or breaking its back.

To obviate this "supporters" were provided to sustain part of the weight. These "cranes" were hinged and were swung in when the boats were lowered.

After a boat was hoisted, the tubs were removed in order to further lighten her.

The tubs were kept on a rack abreast of the boat, inboard, and the preparatory order before lowering was "Get your tubs aboard."

SPARE BOATS

Two spare boats were carried thus on the skids, and were brought into use when one or more of the others were "stove" or destroyed.

Under these spares were racks on which cutting spades and such gear were stowed.

This view is looking forward from the deck over the wheel.

The purpose of the harpoon was not to kill the whale but to be a means of "getting fast" with the whale line.

The killing was done with the lance—a long shanked instrument with a small razor-sharp tip.

From earliest times the whaleman had endeavoured to fashion a harpoon that would not "draw" or pull out. Many variations had been tried of the solid head type of "iron," but they all gave way before the "toggle" iron, invented by a Negro named Lewis Temple in 1848.

The sketch shows only the principal types—and the large variety of bombs and bomb guns has been omitted; they savour too much of modern methods and wholesale slaughter.

A—Two flued iron.   B—Single flued iron.
C—Temple's toggle iron.   D—Modern toggle iron.

In the toggles a wooden match-like pin was inserted through the head of the harpoon to hold it straight. This broke as soon as pull was exerted on the line and the head turned as shown in fig. E.

F— An effective darting gun used against Right and Bowhead whales. A short gun barrel was mounted on the end of the pole. On one side of this was inserted a harpoon attached to the line. Reaching half way to the point was a rod, which on coming in contact with the skin of the whale, exploded the charge in the chamber and discharged a bomb. The whole instrument was thrown in the same manner as a harpoon, the gun-pole being retrieved by a line attached to the boat, the iron remaining in the whale.

Except in the case of lone bulls, guns were of no use among sperm whales; the discharge scared the herd—or as the whaleman said, "gallied the pod."

G—An English double flued iron with "stop withers."

H—The Greener gun—used by Dundee whalers in the Arctic.

J— The harpoon—with slot and travelling ring—fired from the Greener gun.

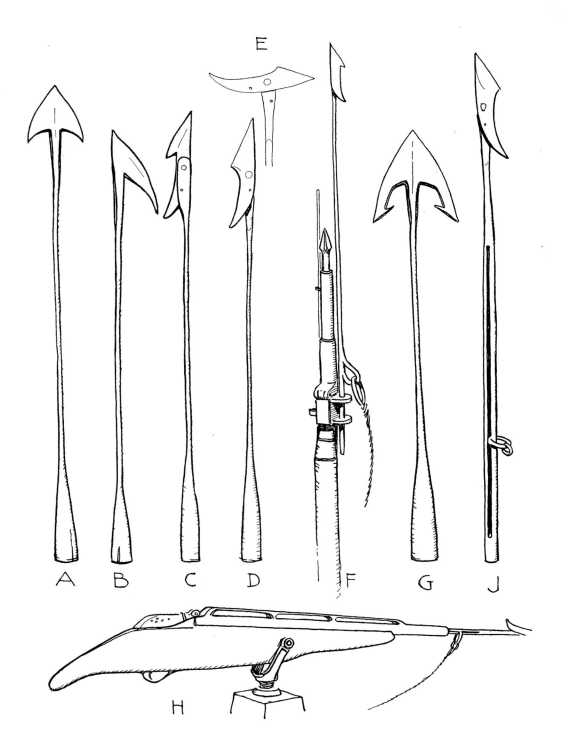

E

A   B   C   D   F   G   J

H

THE WHEEL

THIS type of steering wheel known as "shin cracker" was peculiar to the Yankee whaleships. The wheel was mounted on the tiller and the helm was moved by means of tackle which ran around the drum, through sheaves and blocks to the bulwarks. Consequently, when the steersman turned the wheel he walked back and forward with it across the deck.

In the deck over him there was a small hatch through which he could watch the sails.

THE FOC'S'LE

THE foc's'le was reached by a hatch, forward of the mainmast, which also served as the only inlet for daylight and fresh air.

In some cases the ceiling was so low that any man above average height could not stand upright. In heavy weather the deck was never dry, due to leaky hawse pipes and dripping oilskins, and in the tropics it was a furnace. Altogether, the combined odours of unwashed bodies, unwashed clothes, bilge water, tobacco and oil lanterns, made it a noisome habitation.

The men's bunks were ranged in a double tier along the sides and their sea chests, lashed to the deck, served as benches.

THE WINDLASS

THIS ancient contrivance known as a log windlass was only a slight improvement over its predecessor in which the barrel was laboriously turned by wooden bars or "handspikes" inserted in holes.

In the one shown a ratchet mechanism was added, and when weighing anchor or cutting in a whale, four or five men on each side pumped the brake handles up and down.

One has but to compare this heartbreaking relic to the modern steam or electric winch to appreciate the truth of the captain's allusion to a yachting cruise.

THE GALLEY

HERE the cook, or "doctor" as he was called, prepared the food for officers and crew. The galley was located aft on the starboard side, abreast of the wheel, where the steersman might get an occasional cup of coffee from the cook to ease his trick at the wheel.

How different to the case of the man at the wheel in merchant ships, stamping his feet and blowing on his fingers in the roaring forties, and looking with wistful eyes towards the galley at the far end of the deck.

TYPES

THE crews of Yankee whalers up to, and including, the fifties were made up mostly of Americans drawn from the neighbourhood of the ships' home port.

As the great West opened up, the movement overland diverted the native American from the sea, and in the declining years of the industry crews were composed mainly of Portuguese, Negroes, and Bravas from the Cape Verde Islands.

Whaling crews were not paid wages but were given a "lay," or share in the profits at the end of the voyage.

The lay scale was graded down from 1/16th for the captain to 1/200th for a green hand—and even less to the cabin boy.

At the end of a long voyage, when the ship was credited with oil valued at $250,000, or more, the sailors' share was quite worth while.

THE BLACKSMITH

THE blacksmith's duties lay in the care of all the harpoons, spades, lances, boarding and mincing knives, and kindred gear.

When whales were being killed and brought alongside he was a busy man, straightening and repairing irons, and keeping the cutting-in stage supplied with keen-edged spades.

THE COOPER

WHEN a whaleship set out on a voyage she was loaded from keel to deck with casks of various sizes, from the largest, of fourteen barrel capacity, to long, narrow ones, known as "ryers," used to fill empty spaces and odd corners. Many of them were filled with fresh water to serve as ballast, and all the spare sails, food, clothing (slops) and other reserve articles were headed up in casks.

In due course they were emptied and filled with oil, and the cooper's task was to keep them in good condition, and, if need arose, to construct new ones from the staves, heads and hoops which he had in reserve.

The term "barrel" was only used as a unit of measure:—a cask was spoken of as an eight barrel cask or a whale's size was reckoned in so many barrels.

An average whaler carried in the neighbourhood of five hundred casks of all sizes, and the keeping of them in serviceable condition involved constant watchfulness and work on the cooper's part.

GRINDING SPADES

No ONE was busier than the ship's boy. Helping the steward in the pantry, turning the grindstone, peeling potatoes for the cook, or running aloft to tie stops in the buntlines, he was kept hopping from one job to another.

He doubtless found ere long that whaling was not as romantic a pursuit as he had dreamed it to be, and cried himself to sleep in homesickness many times before the end of the voyage.

COILING LINE TUBS

THE coiling of the whale line in the boats' tubs was a matter demanding extreme care, as not only did the catching of whales depend on the line, but improper coiling might produce sudden kinks and fouling, to result in the maiming or killing of one or more of the crew, or even the loss of the boat itself.

Whale line was made of "long manila fibre" and was three quarters of an inch in diameter. Even when new it was as pliable as an old shoe lace and capable of sustaining a weight of three tons.

In coiling, the line was laid out on deck, the end passed through a snatch block on the mainstay over head, and thence down to the tub. The end, with its eye splice, was left hanging over the edge of the tub where it could be bent onto the second tub should necessity arise.

The line was coiled clockwise to the centre, thence to the side, and the process repeated until the tub was full.

This was known as a "flake" or "Flemish coil."

Each boatsteerer attended to the coiling of his own tubs, a helper meanwhile twisted the line to the left as he pulled it down through the block.

TEN DOLLARS REWARD

IN SOME ships, when whales were scarce, and weeks—even months—elapsed without a kill it was the custom for the captain to have a five or ten dollar gold piece nailed to the mainmast to be claimed by the first man who sighted a "blow."

GRUB

"What's this—the cook's pocketbook?"

Jack always ate his meals on deck except in inclement weather. Salt beef or pork, cooked in a sadly unvarying fashion, was served in small wooden tubs called "kids," and the sailor's treasured privilege, no matter what the quality of the fare might be, was to make uncomplimentary remarks about the cook and all his ancestors.

"FRESH FISH FOR THE COOK TO SPOIL"

In the warmer latitudes there were always fish playing about the ship's bows: bonita, baracouta, dolphins and porpoises——

To vary the weary round of salt "horse" it was no trick at all for one of the boatsteerers to take himself into the martingale stays and bring up a fish that would arouse the envy of any landlubber angler.

WHALES

1—SPERM WHALE. This whale was long avoided by the early whalemen before means were perfected to meet his wary and pugnacious character.

A large sperm whale would measure sixty-five feet and give eighty barrels of oil. Many larger ones have been taken but the average gave forty-five barrels.

Its natural food is the giant squid, which it finds at profound depths—a half mile or more.

Sperm whales are usually found in herds or "pods," except in the case of occasional "lone bulls."

2—RIGHT WHALE. This is the whale of the early history of the industry—docile and easy to take—whose only means of defence lay in its great tail or "flukes." This and the Bowhead were known as "Baleen" or whalebone whales.

They feed on the surface—their food being small crustacea or "brit," which they scoop up with open mouth and strain through the rows of baleen which hang from the upper jaw.

3—BOWHEAD WHALE. The Arctic or Greenland whale. Living in the cold waters of the high latitudes the blubber of this species is much thicker than that of Sperm or Right, one Bowhead rendering as much as three hundred barrels.

The quality of its oil, however, is much inferior to sperm oil, and for years it was hunted for its whalebone alone.

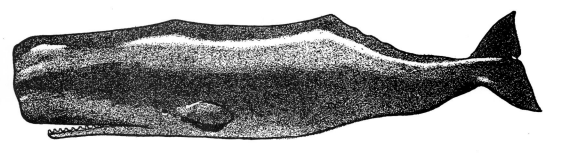

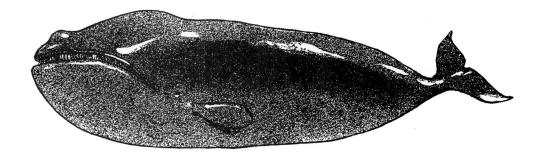

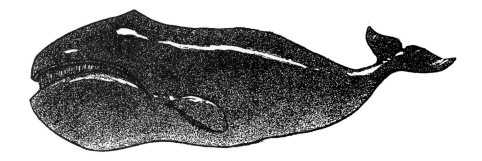

WHALES

4—FINBACK WHALE. This and the Sulphurbottom are much longer than the Sperm, Right, and Bowhead—but were ignored because of the fact that they sank when killed, and because of their rapidity of movement, claimed by some to be as much as fifty miles an hour.

Modern whalers have met these difficulties by employing fast motor boats and by inflating the dead whale with compressed air.

5—SULPHURBOTTOM—or BLUE WHALE. The longest of the whale family. Some specimens have been taken exceeding one hundred feet in length.

6—HUMPBACK WHALE. This whale is one of the "bone" species, but its baleen was too short to be of commercial value.

It sank when killed, but as it was almost always found in shoal water gases due to decomposition brought it to the surface in a short time.

THE MASTHEAD

FROM the day of sailing until the home port was reached at the end of a long voyage, lookouts were always kept at the fore and mainmastheads.

Even with his ship "full to the eyebrows" the whaling skipper could not resist the taking of one more whale, until every possible container, large and small, was full to running over.

The call of the lookout was a sort of wail, running through a scale of five or six notes, each man putting in his own curlicues according to the quality of his voice.

He would sustain the call as long as the blow lasted:

"A blow!—A blo-o-o-o-ow! A blow. A blow!!"

"Where away?" from the skipper.

"Two miles—weather beam—Blo-o-o-ow! Blo-o-o-o-! There she breaches—A blo-o-o-ow! A blow!—A blow!"

LOWERING

THE boats were kept ready for instant lowering. The tubs were first put aboard and a man took his station at each of the "falls" or davit tackles, one man remaining in the boat to fend her off the side of the ship.

"Lower away!"

Down went the boats, the crew following the best way they could, sliding down the falls or scrambling down the side. The hooks were cast off, mast stepped, sail hoisted, and the race for the whale began.

A RACE UNDER SAIL

WHEN the wind was favourable the approach was made under sail.

Various rigs were used: lug, spritsail, and sometimes a jib was set, all designed, however, for quick manipulation.

When sailing, the boat was steered by a rudder; at all other times by the long steering oar.

Meantime the harpooneer was busy with the whale line, running it from the tub, round the loggerhead and forward to the chocks, coiling the "box warp" and attaching his two irons.

WAIFING

WHEN a heavy swell was running it was often impossible for the men in the boats to see the whale, so the lookout at the masthead signalled the direction by means of a flag or "waif."

"GOING ON"

THE angle of vision of the whale was very limited, so the approach was made, if possible, from the right rear, except in the case of a left handed boatsteerer.

On nearing the quarry oars were sometimes replaced by paddles. At the right moment the officer made a sign to the boatsteerer to stand by.

The latter unshipped his oar and looked to his harpoons to see that all was clear.

A second iron was attached by a "short warp" on a running bowline to the whale line, and lay handy, alongside number one.

The boatsteerer did not lift his harpoon and stand poised in readiness. In the excitement attending the crucial moment, he might succumb to buck-fever and be unable to let go.

Instead—he flexed his fingers or rubbed his hands up and down his legs, his eye on the whale, waiting for the command.

"GIVE IT TO HIM!"

LIKE a flash he grasped his iron, and with every ounce of his strength darted it "up to the hitches."

Then the second iron if possible.

If the second could not be used, it was at once thrown overboard, out of the way, to be retrieved later.

SOUNDING

THE instant command was "Stern all!!"—and the boat was backed out of range of the great flaying tail.

Many things might happen in the next few moments.

The whale might "run"—he might turn and attack the boat with open jaws, or "sound."

The boatsteerer and the officer exchanged places.

The line ran out at such speed that water had to be thrown into the tub to prevent the line setting fire to the loggerhead.

A BREACH

SHOULD the whale sound, he would stay down an hour or longer, taking out at times all the line of one or more boats.

If he took all from one and no neighbouring boat was handy to supply more, a wooden contrivance for retarding his speed called a "drug" was made fast to the end of the line and cast loose.

The men peaked their oars, waiting for the whale to reappear.

His reappearance was not a modest drifting to the surface. He was thoroughly enraged, and he came up in a manner dramatic and picturesque.

Suddenly, with the speed of an express train, he rose from the bottom, often making a clean leap out of the water and coming down with a mighty splash.

Lucky the boat's crew that was not caught underneath.

A "CHAWED" BOAT

A FIGHTING bull sperm would often turn and attack the boat, and only the skill of the boatsteerer kept it out of range of the snapping jaws and thrashing flukes.

Boats have been destroyed at one mouthful, and those of the crew as were unable to leap clear. Such was the rage of some whales that they returned again and again to the broken fragments until they were reduced to matchwood.

Gordon Grant

"A NANTUCKET SLEIGH RIDE"

SHOULD the whale run the crew unshipped their oars and faced forward, a turn of the line was made round the loggerhead, and "playing the fish" began. The boat's tub and loggerhead were the equivalent of the reel on the trout fisherman's rod, and the same tactics were employed as in trout fishing, except that the boat followed the whale at a speed of fifteen or more knots an hour.

The boatsteerer snubbed the line by the loggerhead and the crew at each indication of slackening of speed hauled in. Shorter and shorter the line grew as the whale tired, and closer to his flank drew the boat's bow, where the mate stood ready to exercise his time honoured privilege of delivering the final thrust.

A Nantucket sleigh ride, as it was called, often took the boat miles beyond the horizon, and the crew were often obliged to wait many hours, even days, to be picked up by the ship,— indeed in cases of storm or fog there are tragic instances of boats never having been found.

LANCING

To KILL the whale at a single thrust required the greatest skill, and the boat to be laid on at the right spot.

The mate, awaiting the moment when he could reach the "life," made repeated thrusts with his lance in order to weaken the victim.

The success of the final stroke was proclaimed by "spouting red"—and the dying whale went into a "flurry," which consisted of swimming round in a gradually diminishing circle until with a final thrashing of his giant flukes he rolled over on his side "fin out."

TOWING TO THE SHIP

IF MORE whales were in the vicinity, the dead one was "waifed" with a small red flag and the pursuit resumed.

A whale usually ran to windward—leaving the ship far to leeward, shorthanded, and faced with a long beat to pick up her boats.

A line was made fast by a hole cut in the flukes, the boats were connected, and all hands put their backs into the arduous task of towing back to the ship.

CUTTING-IN DIAGRAM

A—Jaw of the Sperm whale

B— Case

C— Junk

D—White Horse

E— Blanket or blubber, which was stripped from the carcass in a spiral fashion. The blubber hook was inserted in a hole, *f*, for the first cut.

G—H—Head and lips of the Bowhead. The latter were very rich in oil.

The same method of stripping was employed in all species of whales.

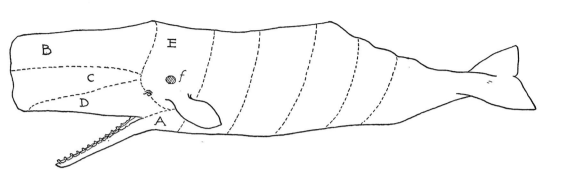

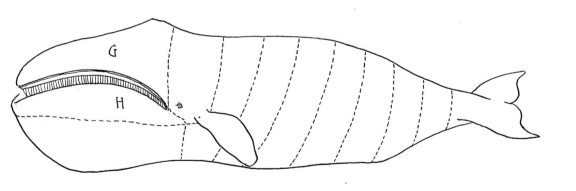

REMOVING THE LOWER JAW
OF A SPERM WHALE

CUTTING in was always done on the starboard side of the ship, and if possible, to windward, so that wind pressure on the sails tended to lift the side of the vessel and sustain the great weight of blubber coming aboard.

The sketch shows the cutting stage rigged out, the huge tackle made fast to the jaw, and the mates on the stage disjointing it with their spades.

The jaw had no commercial value whatever. When a particularly large one was taken, stripped, and dried, it made a picturesque gateway for the captain's garden at home, and the great teeth were used by the crew for their "scrimshaw" work.

THE JUNK

THE jaw having been removed, the junk was then taken off and brought on deck to be cut up and tried out.

The junk was very rich in spermaceti—used by the manufacturers of cosmetics and spermaceti candles.

While the whale lay alongside, the neighbouring waters were infested with a multitude of voracious sharks, which, if the cutting in were not done without delay tore the blubber to shreds.

During cutting in the men on the stage made periodical onslaughts on these robbers with their spades, taking a characteristically seamanlike satisfaction in seeing the wounded sharks instantly set upon and devoured by their fellows.

CUTTING IN

THE captain with the first and second mate, usually was on the stage, taking an active part in cutting in.

The windlass crew were forward, heaving on the tackle which was suspended from the cap of the lower mainmast.

As they hove the blanket rose higher and higher, the cutters plied their spades, and the whale rolled over and over.

THE BLANKET PIECE COMING ABOARD

WHEN the tackle was "block and block," the third mate or one of the boatsteerers, with his "boarding knife," made a hole for the second tackle.

A heavy blubber hook, or the eye in the long strop of the block in the foreground was pushed through and secured on the outside by a heavy wooden pin or toggle.

The second tackle was hove taut to take up the weight and the upper piece sliced off.

LOWERING INTO THE HOLD

As EACH piece was cut off, it was lowered down the main hatch into the blubber room and there cut into "horse pieces," three or four feet long and six or eight inches wide.

MINCING

THE horse pieces were tossed back on deck, where they were placed on a long plank set on tubs and "minced" into "books" or "bible pieces" with large two-handled knives.

The term "books" arose from the fact that the blubber was not cut quite through, and a minced piece bore a rough resemblance to the leaves of a book.

TRYING OUT

DAY and night the try works were kept going, until all the blubber had been rendered.

. Dense black smoke by day, and illuminated sails and rigging at night disclosed to passing ships the proximity of a whaler. Merchant sailors claimed they could smell a "spouter" over the horizon.

The furnace contained two large iron kettles similar to that in the foreground of the sketch. Beneath each of these was a separate fire grate, and under all—a shallow pan of water as safeguard.

The minced blubber was tried out in these kettles, and when the book pieces had given up their oil they were used as fuel. Enough of this "crackling" was kept to start the fires for the next whale.

As the oil filled the kettles, it was bailed off into a copper cooling tank—then to casks on deck where it cooled thoroughly for a day or two before being stowed away in the hold.

BAILING THE CASE

IF THE whale was small, the case was hoisted on deck where it was laid open and the liquid spermaceti saved with scoops and dippers,—but if it was too heavy for this it was secured to the side of the ship, nose end down. A hole was cut into the reservoir and a "case bucket" rigged from the mainyard and manipulated by four men,—one to handle the bucket, two on the guy lines to force it down by means of the pole, and the fourth to hoist and lower.

This oil often amounted to as much as thirty barrels of liquid spermaceti, which had only to be headed up without further treatment.

To this day there has been found no equal to this oil for the lubricating of watches and fine machinery.

CLEANING SHIP

BY THE time the oil was tried out and the stripped carcass cast adrift to make a royal feast for sharks and seabirds, the ship was a slithery mass of oil, gurry, and blood,—to which was added the effects of clouds of smut and black smoke from the try works.

All hands turned to to clean ship. Ashes from the fires were sprinkled on the deck and bulwarks, and brooms and scrubbers were plied until she gleamed again,—except aloft, where the sails hung black and an affront to the eyes of clippermen. When the kettles had been scrubbed inside until they shone like silver punchbowls, the men turned their attention to themselves and their clothes.

To be clean again! How good it felt:—ship, gear, and man.

But how often was it no sooner achieved than a yell from the masthead announced
        "She blows! She blows!"
and all the weary business had to be gone through with again.

MAIN HATCH SURGERY

SOME English and Scottish whalers carried surgeons, but it was not the custom in Yankee ships. Whatever casualties befell his men, the captain attended to as best he could.

Heroic tales are related of bone settings and amputations without anesthetics aboard whaleships that pay high tribute to the fortitude of that vanished race of hardy seamen.

BOAT SURGERY

WHILE the captain repaired his men—"Chips" repaired his boats.

Ships' carpenters received their training as boat builders, and were prepared, not only to mend them, but had "knocked down" parts stowed below for the construction of new ones.

Whaleboats were very lightly built and subjected to extremely rough handling. Seldom did a whaleship start a voyage with anything but new craft on her davits.

ASHORE FOR WATER

As THE casks were filled with oil, the fresh water supply diminished, so shore parties were sent off with empty casks to be filled and towed back to the ship.

HAVING IT OUT

FIGHTING aboard ship was not tolerated by the captain, and grudges were carefully nursed until some shore duty afforded the belligerents an opportunity to settle their affair on the beach.

RECRUITING ON THE BEACH

DISILLUSIONED by hard work, indifferent food, and miserable conditions of living in general, men were constantly deserting the whaleships, especially in the South Seas—where the islands presented a seemingly idyllic existence to the hard driven sailor man.

Whaling captains did their best to repair these losses by recruiting among the beachcombers and deserters from other ships, but the inducements held out were no different to those with which they were only too well acquainted, and met with little success, except in cases where idleness and monotony gave way to a desire to get home again.

Many of these runaways, however, were so steeped in the soft living in the islands that they deserted again at the first opportunity.

A "GAM"

THE tedium of a protracted whale hunt and association with the same companions for months on end was relieved when two ships met at sea. If they hailed from the same port so much the better.

The sails were laid aback, and the captains, mates, and crews exchanged visits. Old friends met, and letters passed—along with newspapers and home gossip. Work ceased—the cook threw a few more raisins in the plum duff—and a general holiday was declared.

A gam might last a day or a week, and if whales appeared there was friendly competition between the boats of one ship and the other, the oil taken during this period of "mating" being shared equally.

SONG AND DANCE

With a Negro or two in the crew, the foc's'le could always be assured of entertainment in the dog watches or during a gam.

BUMBOATS

WHEN ships touched at ports in the Cape Verde Islands, the Azores, or other such rendezvous they were surrounded by peddlers of fresh fruit and vegetables, a very welcome variant after months of salt junk and hardtack.

ARCTIC WHALING

COMPARED to the dramatic action of Sperm whaling, the taking of Right whales was a tame business, but the chase of Bowhead or Arctic whales took men among icebergs and floes where their work was complicated by discomfort and the danger of ships being crushed or wrecked.

Many individual whalers have been thus lost, and in 1871 a fleet of thirty-four was crushed and abandoned in the Arctic ice.

WHALEBONE

WHALEBONE, which once brought a higher price than the oil of the bone whales, has little or no commercial value now.

The sketch shows the upper part of the head of a Bowhead whale, with the whalebone attached.

In larger specimens the slabs of "bone" reached twelve feet or more in length.

CLEANING WHALEBONE

THE "slabs" were cut from the jaw, and after being scraped and washed were tied in bundles.

DEAD MAN'S CHEST

WHEN a man died or deserted, unless the captain chose to take his effects back to his family, they were auctioned off to the highest bidder.

As often as not the chest was worth more than the contents.

HOMEWARD BOUND

INSTEAD of sailing for home when the ship was full, many whalers discharged their oil at the Hawaiian Islands or San Francisco and set out for more.

This oil was put aboard large cargo ships capable of carrying the catch of several whalers, and taken round the Horn to New York, Boston, or the whaleships' home port.

But at last the "spouter" was filled up and ready for the long passage home, the captain served grog, and all hands were hailed aft to "splice the main brace."

"SCRIMSHAW"

WITH a four or five months' passage home before him, the whaleman occupied himself by carving and fashioning all manner of articles out of bone and whales' teeth;—scrimshaw work. He had usually some particular person in mind as he scraped and sawed, filed and drilled, often with tools made from nails or odd bits of metal.—Model ships or boats, knives, forks, combs, ladles, yarn winders, bodkins, and a thousand other nick-nacks were turned out.

The favourite article however was the "jagging wheel,"—a contrivance for decorating pie crust and pastry, and many were the variations on the handles of these jaggers.

The visitor inspecting the fine collection of these what Herman Melville calls "Skrimshandered" articles, in the Nantucket and New Bedford Whaling Museums, cannot help being struck with the exquisite workmanship of most of the specimens and the high degree of artistry attained in the decoration of them.

* * * * * * *

THE whaleman and his trim little ships have gone on the long passage, but if in nothing else, he has left in this a delightful and worthy record behind him.